Two Mothers and Son

a play

Two Mothers and Son

a play

By

Hope Eghagha

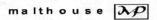

Malthouse Press Limited

Lagos, Benin, Ibadan, Jos, Port-Harcourt, Zaria

©Hope Eghagha 2019
First Published 2019
ISBN 978-978-56219-9-0

Published and manufactured in Nigeria
by

Malthouse Press Limited
43 Onitana Street, Off Stadium Hotel Road,
Surulere, Lagos, Lagos State
E-mail: malthouse_press@yahoo.com
malthouselagos@gmail.com
Tel: +234-802 600 3203

Distributors:
African Books Collective Ltd
Email: abc@africanbookscollective.com
Website: http://www.africanbookscollective.com

Authorial Note

Although the details of this play are essentially fictional, the story-spine is factual. For the purpose of drama I have exercised my poetic licence to significantly alter the denouement and increase the tragic tension of the plot. This I have done to demonstrate a point: any life that is deeply steeped in any form of excessive or pathological control has serious implications for character progression and human development.

I have always been drawn to the strong emotional ties which exist between mothers and their sons, and between a mother and an only son. Once, as a boy my father had playfully observed to me that '*a boy's first love is his mother*', I didn't understand him. For, I grew up in a home where the only love which mattered was Christian love as an obligation. We honoured our parents, the only commandment that carried a promise.

I admired my mother; I loved her commitment to her family, her commitment to her ten children and her husband. She was not partial to any of her ten children! How she was able to achieve this I will leave for another day. But I did not consider the idea of love as that strong, binding force that made a man stick to his mother in a rather fetish way. In my poetry collection *Mama Dances into the Night*, I celebrated my mother and the depth of loss I felt when it dawned on me that the woman who gave me birth was gone forever.

I read D.H. Lawrence's *Sons and Lovers* as an undergraduate and wondered what accounted for the unusual love between Paul and his mother, and how that type of love was capable of strangulating a man, of making a man see only a small picture on the canvas of life. The matriarch of the family invested all her emotions on Paul after she wrote off her miner-husband. I understood the paralysing effect it had on the young Paul and how it later affected his ability to keep relationships, and how he was finally attracted to an older woman who would mother him, as it were. Also one cannot forget Shakespeare's tragic hero Coriolanus in the eponymous drama whose love and weakness for his mother became his undoing.

I have drawn freely from the experiences of others to re-create the character of a possessive mother. There have been mothers who displayed this possessive streak throughout history, in the lives of men. A pick from here and there has given us the dramatic character of Mama Yellow, the central character in the play. In a sense, although Prince Nico Mbarga popularized the image of a mother in his song *"Sweet Mother"*, in the real life not all mothers are sweet.

Hope Eghagha
Lagos NIGERIA
January 2017.

Characters

The Lord Bishop

Onome Atumu – *Son*

Mama Yellow – *Mother*

Ochuko Atumu – *Wife*

Johnny Fasco – *Madam Yellow's nephew*

Martha – *Madam Yellow's sister*

Harriet, Ese, & Andy – *children of the Atumus*

Mosun – *Ochuko's friend*

Eugene – *Mosun's lover*

Jerry – *Atumu's friend*

Tomide - *Barman*

Rev. Father Raymond

Someone-in-the Audience

Crowd

Prelude

(In the Bishop's Court)

BISHOP: Father Raymond, the petition against you is very serious.

FATHER RAYMOND: My Lord Bishop I've known you as a man of fairness, truth and justice and I believe you will give me an opportunity to defend myself.

BISHOP: Of course! The church which I represent stands for the truth; I must follow its paths.

FATHER RAYMOND: I'm grateful my Bishop!

BISHOP: I don't have the details yet. But it states that you, through negative advice and wilful collaboration with sinners, brought tragedy to a rather peaceful and Christian family.

FATHER RAYMOND: All I plead is a listening ear!

BISHOP: That you will get; that you will certainly get! An ear that listens will never lead its owner into trouble.

FATHER RAYMOND: I'm deeply grateful

BISHOP: They have framed charges against you! Wish these old decadent priests would not politicize every issue in the church.

FATHER RAYMOND: I am happy you know them Bishop. Politicians in cassock!

BISHOP: God knows them better! I'm disappointed still.

FATHER RAYMOND: God will settle the issues...

BISHOP: (*Reading from a sheet of paper*) Charge 1: That you interfered with the personal and domestic matters of congregants!

FATHER RAYMOND: I am sure you know that is not possible. They are simply jealous of how many families come to me for counselling because I listen to details about their lives and problems.

BISHOP: Are you telling me?

FATHER RAYMOND: Thank you my Lord

BISHOP: Charge 2: That you assisted a congregant to commit suicide by omission and commission!

FATHER RAYMOND: I took a vow to convert souls, to save lives, not to kill or encourage people to commit suicide.

BISHOP: That you gave negative advice and encouraged wrong actions.

FATHER RAYMOND: My Lord Bishop, nothing can be further from the truth. I did not give negative advice and I did not encourage any wrong action.

BISHOP: Two priests from your Order have endorsed the petition sent in by the family.

FATHER RAYMOND: I can guess who they are.

BISHOP: Your greatest friends in the Mission.

FATHER RAYMOND: I pray for and forgive them.

BISHOP: That's an excellent spirit.

FATHER RAYMOND: If our Lord who did no sin but was condemned to death, and could still pray for his traducers: *"O father, forgive them, for they know not what they do"*. Who am I, a mere sinner not to forgive?

BISHOP: God will vindicate you if this is a mere gang up against you.

FATHER RAYMOND: Amen! That is my strong belief.

BISHOP: It's ridiculous that a priest, who vowed celibacy yet has an allegation of illegally fathering a child against him, has the temerity to raise his voice against anybody.

FATHER RAYMOND: He wants to drag me to the mud with him. You remember the role I played in the matter.

BISHOP: Yes Father Raymond, I remember. There are too many small-minded persons in the ministry of Our Lord these days!

FATHER RAYMOND: It's vengeance time, it's payback time!

BISHOP: I will take some actions, even if temporary to calm frayed nerves and to assure the petitioners that I am for justice.

FATHER RAYMOND: I am for justice too my Bishop.

BISHOP: Very good. Until I hear the details lie low; take a back position.

FATHER RAYMOND: Much obliged Bishop.

BISHOP: You may carry on with Mass; but don't go beyond that for now!

FATHER RAYMOND: I thank The Lord before I thank you for being fair.

BISHOP: It's the Lord's work that we do. You are welcome!

FATHER RAYMOND: I took a vow to serve the Lord all my life, in truth and faithfulness. Therefore if in the course of discharging my duties I make mistakes, I am ready to take the punishment as penance for my misdeeds.

BISHOP: Well said, very well said!

FATHER RAYMOND: But before you take any action, I plead with you to listen to the story which I have to tell.

BISHOP: Go ahead. I'm listening!

The Director's Voice: *A C T I O N!*

(*Sharp Lights Out*)

Act One

Scene One

(The House of the Atumus)

MAMA YELLOW: Onome! (*No response*)
Onome! (*No response still*)
Onome-ooo! What kind of sleep is this that a man cannot hear his own mother? Onome-oooo!

VOICE: What is it? (*Onome opens bedroom door*) Can't I have a moment of sleep in this house? Can't I have sound sleep anymore? What is it mother?

MAMA YELLOW: Is that what you say? *'Can't I have any sound sleep in this house'*?

ONOME: What else to say if you keep banging on my door every night?

MAMA YELLOW: Do I bang on your door every night? A mother hen that does not keep its eyes over its chicks will have to contend with the claws of a hawk.

ONOME: There you go again with your proverbs!

MAMA YELLOW: Did I bang on your door last night?

ONOME: I don't even remember. But it's getting frequent these days.

MAMA YELLOW: Do you think I have nothing to do? Is it not for your sake that I stay up every night, praying, meditating and worrying?

ONOME: You don't have to worry about me. I'm okay; I will be okay.

MAMA YELLOW: It is only at night that I can see you. Besides, it is at night that the mind becomes calm to hear deep things. Isn't that why in the church they keep vigil, praying and crying and singing till the next day?

ONOME: But Mama, you know staying up late affects my energy level and you know I need my energy for the kind of job that I do! By 5am I have to be up, get myself ready along with my wife and children and leave the house by 6.30am so that the kids can get to school early.

MAMA YELLOW: That's what you always say. I can almost repeat your answer.

ONOME: I need my sleep Mama. I need sufficient rest! Or do you want me to break down?

MAMA YELLOW: Break down? You will not break down! Nothing happens to the cubs of *okporhokpo*, the lion!

ONOME: Okay, I will not break down but I need to go back to bed!

MAMA YELLOW: Sleep is the cure to most illnesses; but sleep can also lead to death. Too many people have died while sleeping. Onome, do you know how many nights I went without sleep when I was nurturing you as a baby?

ONOME: Oooo-Mama!

MAMA YELLOW: How I would still wake up early in the morning and make food for your father...

ONOME: Mama!

MAMA YELLOW: ... and for you?

ONOME: I know Mama; you have said it a million times.

MAMA YELLOW: How I would fall ill each time you fell ill!

ONOME: I know Mama!

MAMA YELLOW: How I would stay by your side, ignoring mosquito bites!

ONOME: Mama!

MAMA YELLOW: Ignoring the advice of the doctors that I should get some sleep. I had to stay awake for you to stay alive.

ONOME: I'm grateful...

MAMA YELLOW: How one night because I didn't sleep and when the drip they were infusing you with finished and it started sucking your blood back into the tube!

ONOME: God bless you for your strength and commitment!

MAMA YELLOW: How I saved you once when you convulsed after a high fever!

ONOME: I'm grateful, I'm grateful for all that you did.

MAMA YELLOW: Yes, you have to be grateful! A grateful child will always receive prayers from their parents! It is not the child who got a hundred acres from his father that is a good child; it is the one who makes use of it properly and comes back to say thank you.

ONOME: But you see I came back from work tired and...

MAMA YELLOW: Yes, that's one of the reasons I have come calling. When did you return from work? Why didn't I see you? Have you eaten?

ONOME: Mama, is this why you came to wake me up at midnight?

MAMA YELLOW: I have only one eye; that eye must shine forever!

ONOME: Mama, look at the time!

MAMA YELLOW: Time? What does that mean?

ONOME: Time is money.

MAMA YELLOW: We made time; time did not make us. So let us learn to control time.

ONOME: There is time for everything; even the Bible says so!

MAMA YELLOW: Where I come from, we can talk to our sons at any time of the night or day. There is no fixed time for breast feeding!

ONOME: That was before; not so anymore!

MAMA YELLOW: That is why the world has turned upside down!

ONOME: That is why we don't go late to work!

MAMA YELLOW: That is why you don't spend enough time with your mother!

ONOME: But I need sleep Mama!

MAMA YELLOW: Do you know how many times you woke me up when you were a child at midnight or three in the morning just because you wanted to use the toilet or suck my breast?

ONOME: Mama, I know...

MAMA YELLOW: Look at my skin. I'm not as light in complexion as I used to be. Why was I named Mama Yellow? Because of my complexion! But when I started trading and facing the harshness of life, I lost my complexion.

ONOME: Yes, they said to me that you were very beautiful.

MAMA YELLOW: You can say that again. It was my beautiful yellow skin that made your father fall in love with me. He treated me with care and caution like an egg. He so petted me that the others were jealous. He used to call me 'my oyibo'.

ONOME: You are still beautiful Mama!

MAMA YELLOW: Do you know how many times I slept on my feet just to make sure you were okay Onome?

ONOME: Mama you have said this before...

MAMA YELLOW: Do you know how many prayer houses I took you to, to cover you with the blood of Jesus? How many times you almost died in my arms and I would suck the mucus in your nostrils to breathe life into you again?

ONOME: I was small and helpless then. You see Mama...

MAMA YELLOW: I am now old and helpless. So what makes it wrong for you to support me?

ONOME: Nothing Mama, nothing.

MAMA YELLOW: I rang the bell for you when you stepped into the world; it is your turn to ring the bell and carry me into the night of my life!

ONOME: Okay Mama, you win. Now, what's the matter this time?

MAMA YELLOW: That's my son. Come; sit down. Let's talk.

ONOME: It must be serious for you to wake me up at such an odd hour!

MAMA YELLOW: I am happy to have a son I can talk to and chat with any time that I like. God bless you. Besides, as one gets older, sleep becomes more difficult to find. It is as if one is afraid of closing the eyes for too long so that it does not remain permanent.

ONOME: Okay Mama. What is this talk about?

MAMA YELLOW: What time did you return from work today?

ONOME: It was quite late. Around 10.30pm.

MAMA YELLOW: What kept you so late?

ONOME: What else but work?

MAMA YELLOW: Are you sure?

ONOME: I don't understand!

MAMA YELLOW: Or did you sneak to the house of that beautiful light-skinned beauty that I introduced to you?

ONOME: (*Standing up*) Mama, please don't start. You know I will never do that.

MAMA YELLOW: Sit down, sit down. What is it? Getting angry easily like your father!

ONOME: It's late and I have to get enough sleep so I can wake up early tomorrow morning. You know how Lagos is!

MAMA YELLOW: Did they give you food to eat when you returned from work? I have some soup, delicious *banga* soup with dry fish and snails, which you love so much. I prepared it myself. Not that watery stuff that they give you.

ONOME: Mama! I'm okay. I'm okay. I've had dinner.

MAMA YELLOW: Are you really okay? Tell me. How was work today?

ONOME: Work was hectic as usual. But you see, the economy is shaky and all hands have to be on deck. We must work hard so the company does not fold up.

MAMA YELLOW: Nothing will happen to your job my son. Anyone who tries to trouble you will eat sand and pass out blood in public! Anyone who tries to shake the *Iroko* can only shake himself; not the tree!

ONOME: Maaaama!

MAMA YELLOW: You are my only son; my only portion on this earth as God has allowed it to be. I can't question him. Nothing bad must happen to you. You will rise from glory to glory!

ONOME: Amen Mama. May I go to bed now?

MAMA YELLOW: Go to bed? Why? I haven't started the matter!

ONOME: What is the issue now?

MAMA YELLOW: It's the same matter I told you about before. I had a dream last night.

ONOME: Have you become Mama the Dreamer?

MAMA YELLOW: Your father appeared to me and asked whether you have built a house.

ONOME: My father?

MAMA YELLOW: Yes, the dream was very clear, just like a movie...

ONOME: Why didn't he appear to me? Why must it be you?

MAMA YELLOW: Do you doubt me? Doubt my dream?

ONOME: If he is my father and he wants to pass a message across to me, why go through a third party?

MAMA YELLOW: Am I a third party?

ONOME: Yes, between us, between my father and me you are a third party.

MAMA YELLOW: What do you mean?

ONOME: I mean why should he come to you?

MAMA YELLOW: He was my husband, and your father; he was the link between us and I am the link between both of you.

ONOME: He knows better than to appear to me in any dream, that is, if he is actually the one showing up in your dreams.

MAMA YELLOW: What do you mean?

ONOME: What do I mean?

MAMA YELLOW: Yes. What do you mean by '*if he is really the one showing up in your dreams*!

ONOME: Oh that? It could be your conscious mind playing on your subconscious and unconscious. It is what you want that comes to you in your dreams!

MAMA YELLOW: And if he appears to you in your dreams, what would you do?

ONOME: If he appears to me? Hmm! I would tell him some hard truths about life.

MAMA YELLOW: Like what?

ONOME: You want to hear?

MAMA YELLOW: Yes

ONOME: You really want to hear?

MAMA YELLOW: *(No answer)*

ONOME: Question 1! Why did he marry a young girl a third or fourth wife when he was already old and fathered me when he knew he won't be around to look after me?

MAMA YELLOW: Onome!

ONOME: You want to hear? So hear it all. Question 2! Is it not irresponsible for a 70yr old man to bring a child into the world, knowing that he could die any time? That he might not be around to be a real dad?

MAMA YELLOW: But I brought you up…

ONOME: Yes, you brought me up and it is a sing song now in the house. It has become a leash which you tie me with.

MAMA YELLOW: Don't talk like this…

ONOME: Like how? You think you are the only one that has a memory?

MAMA YELLOW: This is not why I called you…

ONOME: Do you know what it is like growing up without knowing your dad, without having a memory of him?

MAMA YELLOW: Onome, please listen to me…

ONOME: Who did I learn fatherhood from? I had to read books on how to be a dad when all my peers did was to copy from their father. You know what that means?

MAMA YELLOW: When you start talking like this, I just don't know what to say…

ONOME: Don't say anything. Both of you did enough damage.

MAMA YELLOW: Damage? Damage for bringing you into the world?

ONOME: Yes, you too took a selfish decision.

MAMA YELLOW: Selfish decision Onome? Selfish how?

ONOME: Yes; bringing up a child is the responsibility of two people. And if one of them already knows, after having over twelve kids by three women that he might not be around for long, it is selfish to bring another child into the world.

MAMA YELLOW: Isn't that why he keeps showing up in my dreams, to guide you?

ONOME: What's his business whether I have built a house or not?

MAMA YELLOW: Onome!

ONOME: Why did he cut me out of his will?

MAMA YELLOW: He didn't...

ONOME: Why didn't he leave me a house in his will?

MAMA YELLOW: You have to understand what really happened.

ONOME: Why did he give everything to the children of his first wife?

MAMA YELLOW: Your father meant well...

ONOME: No Mama. Don't bring him into this matter. If that is why you have woken me up let me go back to bed now.

(Door opens. Silence. Ochuko comes out in her night dress. Walks across to the kitchen)

MAMA YELLOW: Be patient my son; be patient. In this life, the cup of water meant for you can never pass you by. Any cap designed for your head will return to you even if it travels one thousand kilometres away. Whatever belongs to your mouth can never be snatched away by any other person and put inside another mouth. When an ailment is stubborn it is bitter medicine that we use to cure it. What is sweet is sweet and what is bitter is bitter. The mouth that eats sweet things is the same mouth that eats bitter things. But it is the sweet things that we want, that we pray for. Birds have no visas but they can travel to any country of their choice.

(*Kitchen door opens. Ochuko is returning from the kitchen with a glass of water. Stops when she gets to the bedroom door*)

OCHUKO: Onome darling, I'm waiting for you. Let us finish what we started!

ONOME: I will be with you shortly, darling!

MAMA YELLOW: You should know that I have unfinished business with my son too!

OCHUKO: Mama, it's almost two in the morning. Let my husband go to bed please!

MAMA YELLOW: I must have this talk with MY son, if you don't mind.

OCHUKO: I want MY husband in the room Mama!

MAMA YELLOW: Shameless woman! Aren't you tired of those things?

OCHUKO: I'm not tired of those things. I'm tired of having a mate in the house!

MAMA YELLOW: What did you say?

ONOME: Ochuko, please!

OCHUKO: It's the time I am looking at, honey! It's late; you have to go to work early.

MAMA YELLOW: Mind your business!

OCHUKO: My husband is my business Mama!

MAMA YELLOW: My son is my business. Thank you Miss Caretaker!

OCHUKO: Just know that I have a mother too.

MAMA YELLOW: If you had a mother, you wouldn't insult me!

OCHUKO: I didn't insult you. But this hatred you have for me; it's only God that will reward you!

ONOME: Please Ochuks, don't exchange words with my mother; don't let her provoke you. I will soon join you in the room.

(Gives Mama a nasty look and shuts the door)

MAMA YELLOW: That is how they will insult me in your house and you won't say anything.

ONOME: She didn't insult you.

MAMA YELLOW: Did she not say God will punish me?

ONOME: No, she said no such thing.

MAMA YELLOW: It's okay-o! There are times when without being told, you somehow know that your mouth has an odour!

ONOME: Nobody has talked about an odour! But if I know my mouth has an odour I would wash it three times a day!

MAMA YELLOW: Our people say you insult a deaf man by giving the abuse to his son!

ONOME: I've got to go to bed now Mama!

MAMA YELLOW: Why? Is it because your wife has come to wink her eyes and shake her buttocks at you?

ONOME: Maaama! Please stop this!

MAMA YELLOW: Stop what?

ONOME: You are making life difficult for me!

MAMA YELLOW: You are abandoning me because of that woman!

ONOME: Abandoning you for that woman? My wife? How? Have I not accommodated you for over ten years now?

MAMA YELLOW: So that is a big thing *enh*? Everybody come and hear-oo! It is a big thing that I am staying in my son's house!

ONOME: It's not a big thing. It is my duty to look after you. But Mama why do you make life hard for everybody?

MAMA YELLOW: Make life hard for everybody? How?

ONOME: You pick a quarrel with my wife every day!

MAMA YELLOW: That one? Was she there when my water burst and you came into the world?

ONOME: Maama!

MAMA YELLOW: That is what you will say: *Maama*! Was she there when I nursed you? Was she there when you were circumcised? When you bled for two days? Was she there? Was she there when I sent you to school? Was she there? When you had a serious eye infection that almost made you blind? Was she there?

ONOME: She wasn't there, Mama. She was not there. She was being nursed by a mother too! A mother like you! Remember she is somebody's daughter, somebody who loves her as you love me. Why don't you take her as one of your daughters, as a daughter you didn't have?

MAMA YELLOW: But she is not my daughter. She is another woman's daughter.

ONOME: I know she's not your biological child. Motherhood is a mental thing; it is a thing of the mind.

MAMA YELLOW: *(Almost in tears)* But my only daughter, my own blood was killed!

ONOME: That is why you should take my wife like your daughter and live in peace with her. If you love me it's enough to make you love the woman that I love; a woman who has given us three healthy children.

MAMA YELLOW: She has given you three children, not me.

ONOME: Are my kids not yours?

MAMA YELLOW: They are your kids. They are my grandchildren. There is a difference between your own child and a grandchild!

ONOME: Maaama! That's an unfair thing to say!

MAMA YELLOW: Is there fairness in this world? Answer me! Is this world fair? Look here, when your father died, I was a complete housewife. I had nothing. He left nothing for me because the other wives played me out. I was a young girl, forced into marrying an old man by my parents. I had no choice. When he died, I looked up to heaven, nothing was forthcoming. I could not use my certificate to work. All our male in-laws just wanted to inherit the young wife, sleep with her and make children in your father's name. I refused. So I was sent packing from the family house. Are you still talking about fairness?

ONOME: I know they were not fair. I have heard all this before. Why again this night?

MAMA YELLOW: Because you seem to have forgotten that I am your mother! Don't interrupt me any longer.

ONOME: Yes ma!

MAMA YELLOW: I went into the fishing trade. Do you know what that means? To trade in fish! I would go to the creeks, meet fishermen as they came from the deep waters. Sometimes they would sell to me on credit; sometimes they would refuse. I would stay there for days, sometimes weeks to allow the fish to dry. I would then return by boat, give to my customers and make another trip. During the nights, I would sit-sleep. Do you know what that means? To sit inside the rocking boat inside troubled waters and sleep. Some nights pirates would attack us, rape women and steal our goods. Thank God they never came near me for that kind of nonsense. I would have cut off somebody's penis before they killed me. Poor women who had borrowed money would lose everything to pirates. There were times I went without food for days because I didn't want to eat into my capital. I did all of that for you, so you could go to university. Now that you have graduated and become somebody, I am nothing to you, my mouth smells.

ONOME: You are everything to me. Don't you talk like this! Is that why you will not play with my children? Aren't they your children too?

MAMA YELLOW: They are that woman's children. You are the only one that I have.

ONOME: Please Mama, don't utter those words ever. Do let those words get into the ears of people. They will call you names that you will regret forever!

MAMA YELLOW: They don't behave like my children? Anything I say, they go and tell her and she makes faces at me. Are those my kids? Would my kids do that to me? I know she doesn't want me in this house.

ONOME: She wants you; everyone wants you but when you get so difficult and quarrelsome, everyone feels that things would be better if you had your own place.

MAMA YELLOW: Including you *abi?* You want me to go too, don't you? You want me to leave you and your wonderful *peperempe* in the house *abi*? It is well. If that is how to treat your mother who suffered for you, God will judge. Just remember that I may not have many shiny, new clothes; but when it comes to rags, you and your wife have not been born!

ONOME: Mama, I think we have had enough for one night. Allow me to go to bed. Please. I will see you in the morning before I leave.

MAMA YELLOW: It's alright son. *To de!*

ONOME: Good night Mama. *Migwo*!

MAMA YELLOW: *Vren doh*! Goodnight.

(*Onome leaves the stage and enters his bedroom*)

MAMA YELLOW: Listen to me good people of the land. In my next life, I will not be a second wife to anybody. I will not come from a poor family. I will start life early. I will not marry an old man. I will marry a man my age. I will not have only one child. I will have ten children so that nobody can hold me to ransom. I will have boys and girls and educate all of them. You young girls listening to me, do not let anybody sweet talk you into polygamy, into sharing your husband with different women. It is a dreadful thing. See what has befallen me in my son's house!

SOMEONE-IN-THE-AUDIENCE: Na who send you before?

MAMA YELLOW: I no blame you. I blame your Mama wey no born you well.

SOMEONE IN THE AUDIENCE: Nor curse my Mama-o!

MAMA YELLOW: I no blame you. Na condition make crayfish bend!

(Sharp lights out)

24

Act One
Scene Two

(The Atumus' House. When the scene starts, the dialogue had already commenced. Johnny Fasco and Aunty Martha are visiting. Both Johnny's dressing and word-articulation and accent reflect his many years in America.)

MAMA YELLOW: I don't understand this *yeye, yamayama* story you are telling me. Are you saying because you slapped your own wife you were sent out, deported from America?

JOHNNY FASCO: Damn it, aunty, damn them; the bloody racists kicked me out like a common criminal men. It's not cool at all Mama, not cool.

MAMA YELLOW: Just like that? Are you sure? Are you sure you didn't kill somebody, you didn't steal, you didn't take somebody's wife?

JOHNNY FASCO: I can swear that that's the truth, and nothing but the truth Mama! What am I gonna do with another man's woman? I got no business killing nobody. I love life Mama. I really love the good life. Can't harm a soul Mama!

MARTHA: When he told me the story, I didn't believe it at all. How could a girl whom we arranged from here, a girl we picked from the road of poverty, send my son out of

America? This world is becoming something else. How can a man be deported from a country because he beat up his wife, a wife that he married and trained with his money?

MAMA YELLOW: You mean a woman can sack a man from their own home?

JOHNNY FASCO: Aunty, the laws in America favour women against men. I have many friends who have suffered the same fate in the last ten years Mama. My friend Dike brought a young lady from Nigeria, and put her through nursing school. After graduation, she got a job and started to earn big money. She then lost all respect; I mean the bitch, lost all respect for her husband. She would return late to the house and ask the man to prepare his meals. She was always tired at night. She then filed for a divorce and the man was asked to move out of their matrimonial home.

MAMA YELLOW: God forbid!

JOHNNY: God forbid? I'm afraid that though America is God's own country they do not forbid taboos that we all know. O yes. He was forced out. He got another apartment while the divorce proceedings were on. When he got wind of a hot affair going on between his wife and another man, he visited the house. The lover and his wife were making out in his bedroom. They didn't even lock the door. He blasted both of them whack whack dead and called the police.

AUNTY MARTHA: Served them right! Adultery right on their matrimonial bed! Abomination!

JOHNNY: As we speak Mama Dike is in gaol, sentenced to twenty years in prison without an option of parole.

MAMA YELLOW: That can't happen here. God forbid. How can a wife send her husband packing from the house that he built?

AUNTY MARTHA: Who is looking after their children?

JOHNNY: They are in the hands of the State man, ready for foster care! Damn it man!

MAMA YELLOW: How could that happen? How could they just send you away from your children just like that?

JOHNNY: You see, it's a complex situation Mama. Life and things in the States are very different from life here. That was the first shock I got when I arrived there many years ago.

MARTHA: Let John tell you the full story.

MAMA YELLOW: Is there a story?

JOHNNY: Yeah, auntie. A god damn long story! A story that I often don't want to remember. It sure brings tears to my eyes. My kids I don't see no more. They were turned against me by their mother; their mother whom I sent through nursing school. Now they don't even write to me. They won't take my calls. Did I become a monster overnight? I ask myself. It all started three years ago. I took ill. I came down with diabetes. I couldn't work anymore. I was paid my severance benefits which didn't amount to much; the company claimed to have spent a lot of money on my health. My mother-in-law arrived in the States about this time. She came on a visit, at least that's what they told me. But gradually, it turned out to be a permanent stay. She started running the house.

MAMA YELLOW: What do you mean by 'she started running the house?

JOHNNY: At the time she arrived, we were both still working. Each day we left the house for work, we were happy that we had a dependable person looking after the kids. Gradually she started doing the shopping; we started giving her the monthly allowance for shopping. It was so convenient. Then I became ill. She showed interest, looking after me like her own son. Then I lost my job. Aunty Yellow, I lost my manhood. It was as if the past never existed. They started treating me like dirt. I would get food once in a day. When I complained my wife would say that all the monies in the house were going into fees and groceries and bills. The situation degenerated and we started having incessant quarrels. We had both verbal and physical fights and each time we fought the social services people and the police would say I was wrong. Once they arrested me and a judge warned me to be of good behaviour or I would be barred from going to the house.

MAMA YELLOW: A judge said that in this world?

MARTHA: Be patient sister; you haven't heard the rest of the story.

JOHNNY: Sheye, my wife then moved into a separate bedroom. We became strangers in the house. She and her mother and the kids would carefully avoid me in the house. They had their meals while I was asleep. Sometimes I would wake up hungry and go to the kitchen just to take a bite and the kitchen would be locked. So we had a big fight, a very big one. I threw her mother through the window, and gave Sheye a good beating. I was detained and charged to court. While I was in court, Sheye wrote to Immigration that I had entered the country twenty-three years ago with a forged identity, that the certificates I had used to secure a job belonged to my late brother. They investigated and concluded that she was right. From there I was taken to the airport and out on the next available plane.

MAMA YELLOW: How could a mother-in-law create so much trouble in her daughter's home and break a marriage?

OCHUKO's Voice echoes: My mother used to say *"what happened in sheep's house will happen in goat's house"*

MAMA YELLOW: That cannot happen in my son's house!

MARTHA: God forbid. *Oyibo* people have spoiled the world with their *yeye* human rights campaign!

MAMA YELLOW: Is that the country where a man can marry another man?

MARTHA: The land where two women can marry and a man can change himself into a woman!

JOHNNY: I have no quarrel with two men or two women getting married. I will never do it; but I won't judge them. The one that kicks my guts is how much power to have given to women, to wives. It's the so-called feminism that has confused the world. They claim that men and women are equal in marriage. But the way laws are enforced, women have more rights than men. The marshals didn't even let me get to my house to get my personal things. They have ruined me. They didn't allow me get to my computer, my box of clothes, you know. Where do I start from? Unfair Mama, very unfair. Where am I gonna start from?

MAMA YELLOW: It's alright. As long as there is life, there is hope. Just settle down and start a new life. As a *been-to*, you will find hundreds of ladies who want to marry and look after you. With their own money, they will organize the wedding and make everything look good.

MARTHA: I've advised him not to worry. But he keeps talking about America and going back to fight it out. That's why I brought him to see you.

JOHNNY: Do you think I wanna sink into that? Make a woman marry me and turn me into her property? I'm not gonna stand for that, never gonna monkey around women who have the financial muscle to make a fool of me!

MAMA YELLOW: Young man, take things easy. We are women and what we are telling you is the truth. Life is very different here. You have been away for too long. Wives are still loyal and supportive here. (*Hoot of a car*) I think the children have returned from school.

(*Three children run in, with their school bags strapped to their backs*)

CHILDREN: Good afternoon granny.

MAMA YELLOW: Welcome

CHILDREN: Good afternoon auntie and uncle!

MARTHA: Children, meet Uncle John my son!

HARRIET: Welcome uncle.

JOHNNY: Thanks

ESE: Are you the one who lives in America?

JOHNNY: I used to live in America.

ANDY: Why did you come back home? Life is better in America.

MAMA YELLOW: That's how you people ask big big questions!

JOHNNY: It's okay aunty. Kids will always ask questions. Yeah, I came back because of some issues. I will go back once they are resolved.

ANDY: I will go with you to America!

JOHNNY: That's okay; welcome back from school. How was school today?

HARRIET: School was great.

JOHNNY: Any homework?

HARRIET: Yes I have some assignments to do.

JOHNNY: Cool. How old are you young lady?

HARRIET: I'm fifteen.

ESE: Yes. I will work on my assignment after lunch.

JOHNNY: What's your age?

ESE: I'm twelve years old.

JOHNNY: That's cool.

MARTHA: Good children. Welcome back. Have a great day.

MAMA YELLOW: It's alright now. Go and get ready for lunch.

CHILDREN: Thank you granny.

(*They leave the sitting room for their rooms*)

JOHNNY: Beautiful kids. I miss my kids like hell.

MAMA YELLOW: Nothing fantastic about them. From now, let's mind our tongue. These little devils will reveal everything you say to their mother when she returns.

JOHNNY: But we are not discussing anything injurious to anybody! Nothing we have said here will offend anybody Mama!

MAMA YELLOW: You won't understand Johnny, you won't understand.

MARTHA: I guess it's time to leave. Thanks for your listening ears

MAMA YELLOW: I thank you too for coming to see me. John I'm happy you came to see me.

JOHNNY: It's a pleasure aunty.

MARTHA: My two grand children will be back from school now. I need to be home to prepare their lunch.

MAMA YELLOW: Are you their cook?

MARTHA: They are my children. I can do anything to please them. They just make me happy. Every time I look at them I remember when their father was a kid.

MAMA YELLOW: Aren't you lucky?

MARTHA: I thank God everyday for my grandchildren.

MAMA YELLOW: (*Seeing her visitors off*) Johnny just remain strong, okay? Everything will be alright.

JOHNNY: I got no choice. I will do my best to stay strong and fight to return to America to see my children.

(*As soon as the visitors leave, the three kids return to the sitting room and march into the kitchen to warm their food. As they re-enter the stage with their individual plates, Mama Yellow stands up to leave*)

HARRIET: Granny where are you going?

MAMA YELLOW Are you a police woman now?

HARRIET: I just wanted to know why you are leaving the sitting room.

MAMA YELLOW: Thank you; what's your name by the way?

ESE: Granny, don't tell me you don't know her name?

HARRIET: My name is Harriet.

MAMA YELLOW: Harriet, just mind your business.

HARRIET: Ok, granny.

(She leaves)

ESE: Why is Granny so hostile to us?

ANDY: Is she not our father's mother? Why does she behave to us as if we are enemies?

HARRIET: She does not like our mommy. She only loves daddy.

ANDY: She does not really love daddy. If she really loved daddy, she would love us her grandchildren too.

ESE: Sometimes I greet her and she won't even answer.

HARRIET: That is not new. Has she not given you a knock on your head before for no reason? She would then say *'why are you looking at me like that?*

ESE: I hate her. I hate the way she treats mommy and dad will just do nothing.

HARRIET: Will my mommy be like granny when she is old? Would she hate my children, hate my husband?

ANDY: I look forward to when she will leave this house.

HARRIET: Amen. That one! She will never leave.

ESE: Our mommy will never be like that. Not all grannies are wicked. You need to see the way Jite's grandmother pampers him.

ANDY: Yes, I've witnessed it. All four kids in that house even prefer their granny to their mother.

ESE: Wish our granny could just change a bit.

HARRIET: The only thing that can free us from her is death!

ESE & ANDY: Ahhhhhhhhhhhhh! Harriet!

ESE: It's not good to wish anybody dead!

(*The hoot of a car catches their attention*)

ANDY: That must be daddy

ESE: And mommy too

(*Mr. & Mrs. Atumu arrive*)

The Children: Welcome daddy!

Welcome mommy!

How was your day?

 Did you go and pick mommy from the office?

ONOME: So many questions at the same time. How have you been? How was school today?

OCHUKO: Any home work?

ONOME: I can see you are having dinner. Give us a few minutes to unwind and we will come back to the sitting room. Where is granny?

HARRIET: She is in her room; she left here not too long ago.

(*As if on cue, granny's room door opens*).

ONOME: *Migwo* Mama!

MAMA YELLOW: *Vre.* Welcome back my son. How was work?

ONOME: Work was fine. How are you?

MAMA YELLOW: I thank God.

OCHUKO: *Migwo* Mama!

MAMA YELLOW: *Vre.* How was work?

ONOME: Work was hectic as usual but I thank God

OCHUKO: Let me change to my house clothes and get dinner ready.

ONOME: Mama, I will see you later. Let me rest, get some food.

(Ochuko has left; she is in front near their bedroom door. Onome is still talking to his mother)

MAMA YELLOW: Are you sure you will have time to talk today?

OCHUKO: Darling, please come to the room to relax and see Mama later.

MAMA YELLOW: I hope they didn't stress you too much in the office?

ONOME: I am very fine.

MAMA YELLOW: Aunty Martha came visiting while you were away.

ONOME: Really? Hope everything is alright!

MAMA YELLOW: Yes. She came with John her son who was deported from America.

ONOME: A sad story.

MAMA YELLOW: That rubbish can't happen in our country.

ONOME: Of course not......

MAMA YELLOW: It cannot happen in this house. My son would you let that happen?

ONOME: What are you talking about Mama? Let's live in peace and be happy in the house. The laws in America protect the wives from being harassed by family or by the husband. For that reason, any time there is a conflict between the man and the woman, it is the man that the law kicks out, leaving the wife and kids in the house.

OCHUKO's VOICE FROM WITHIN: Darling! Do come and change into your house clothes! You can hear the stories after your dinner!

MAMA YELLOW: The white people have spoiled the world!

ONOME: Some overbearing people are destroying families without knowing it.

MAMA YELLOW: No wife should be overbearing!

ONOME: Nobody Mama should be overbearing in any family!

OCHUKO's VOICE: Sweeeeety!

(He flops into a seat in exasperation)

Sharp Lights out

Act One

Scene Three

(Scene takes place in Mosun's apartment. There is a knock or a
bell rings. Mosun answers from within. She comes into
the living room to welcome her guest)

MOSUN: Who is it?

VOICE: Guess by my voice.

MOSUN: I'm not ready for any stupid games today. Whoever
you are, if you are not ready to identify yourself please
try the next door.

VOICE: Okay...okay...It's me Eugene. *(She opens the door.*
Eugene sweeps in and tries to hug her. She shrugs him
off. He finally succeeds in catching up with her. A hug)

EUGENE: Why are you grumpy on a day as sweet as this?

MOSUN: What is sweet about the day?

EUGENE: Any day that you wake up hale and hearty sweet! So
you must enjoy it darling!

MOSUN: It's been a rough day for me; I'm up this minute and
the next minute my spirit drops.

EUGENE: My baby, what is the matter? You have always been
strong and cheerful. Come on...

MOSUN: I can't remember now the name of the musician who sang *"I've got scars that cannot be seen"*.

EUGENE: That type of scar never heals. But you must never give in to sorrow my dear! The future belongs to those who believe; those who hope in spite of the haze of today.

MOSUN: I am sad; I hardly can place my finger on why. It's as if I carry a heavy burden that is weighing me down.

EUGENE: The country carries a burden right now that weighs it down; and it can affect individuals too.

MOSUN: You are right; we make up the nation and when the nation ails, it affects us too. But mine has a personal dimension to it. There are certain things I want to do, certain decisions I want to make. But somehow I don't have the will power to do them.

EUGENE: Don't worry; things will improve soon. Okay? But tell me; is there something you want me to do? Just mention it my sweet baby and it will be done! You want to change your car, or you want to move into a bigger apartment?

MOSUN: Nothing materialistic Eugene. It's deeper than that.

EUGENE: Now! Now! Now! What is it that troubles you so deeply? Since I came in here today, there have been no words of endearment. It's unlike you. Looks like you are deeply troubled my dear.

MOSUN: Not really. I mean, it's okay. I can manage.

EUGENE: Are you sure?

MOSUN: I am sure, very sure. *(Changing the topic)* You are welcome to my home. How was your day?

EUGENE: My day was turbulent. Between the Police and Customs I don't know which I should report to God first. The day started off well; but when I got to the port, they put ashes in my mouth.

MOSUN: Sorry oo!

EUGENE: That was after policemen had harassed me on the road, asking for all the impossible things on earth. In the last encounter, I didn't know whether to laugh or get angry. The policeman had asked for all my particulars including documents which the IG had specifically told the nation that the police have no business with. After staring at me for a few seconds, he asked me what I had in the boot of the car. I said nothing. He then said, '*so you don't have a spare tyre? Let's go to the police station.* I opened the boot and he saw the spare tyre and other car items. 'Next time", he said, "you must give the police accurate information". He strutted off after delaying me for over one hour.

MOSUN: You were delayed because you failed to understand or play the game.

EUGENE: Which is?

EUGENE & MOSUN: Failing to parting with money!

(They both laugh)

EUGENE: The Customs guys showed me pepper.

MOSUN: How?

EUGENE: I was supposed to clear my goods today. You remember those used cars which my business counterpart sent to me from America?

MOSUN: Yes, you talked about twenty or so cars to be cleared and sold.

EUGENE: After making payments at the bank as I was directed, I got to the Customs Office at the port only to be told that the import duty for used cars has gone up by 100%!

MOSUN: No! It seems this government does not want the poor people to drive cars in their lifetime!

EUGENE: Sad. Judging by the way things are going, the average worker will wait for a long time to afford the simple necessities of life!

MOSUN: Most people could not afford rice last December. Chicken and turkey cost twice more than they used to be!

EUGENE: It's the exchange rate of our currency to the dollar and the wild statements credited to the President that caused the price hike.

MOSUN: No, it's corruption; that is what the government says.

EUGENE: There has always been corruption in this country, but things never got this bad.

MOSUN: Whatever they do, they should remember the common man.

EUGENE: The uncertainty in regulations and rules affects business badly. You wake up with one policy and go to bed with a new policy, often at variance with pre-existing contractual obligations. I don't know how long this will go on for.

MOSUN: I don't know. It's particularly tough on businessmen.

EUGENE: How was your own day?

MOSUN: I went to work, came back early. In the office there was not much work to do. I've been in the house since then. I'm expecting Ochuko.

EUGENE: Really? Hope there are no issues between you?

MOSUN: None that I know of. Eugene, I'm tired of this life.

EUGENE: Tired? What do you mean?

MOSUN: This relationship is getting us nowhere. I think we should review it.

EUGENE: What has happened again?

MOSUN: Nothing has happened. As you know, I'm not getting younger. We've been together for five years now. It's clear that you cannot marry me. Why should I keep hanging on?

EUGENE: I am sure you were hurt by somebody in the office. What is the matter my sweet big baby?

MOSUN: Listen Eugene! It's not a question of being hurt in the office. It's the fact of being inside a state of permanent hurt, the fact that my future can't be with you yet you keep holding me down!

EUGENE: What are you driving at? Have you found another man? Has somebody been feeding your mind with rubbish?

MOSUN: Hmmm! Is that what comes to your mind? Another man? I'm surprised you don't really know me, that you have not really bothered to know the real me. Well, I have been a toy to you. Does anyone ever try to understand a toy?

EUGENE: May be you are tired with me and want to move on and you have met another guy.

MOSUN: I haven't met another man; but I think it is time I stopped fooling myself.

EUGENE: Mosun dear, come on. We can always resolve things!

MOSUN: If as a lover of five years you cannot meet my mother then I should have a re-think.

EUGENE: But you didn't allow me to meet your mother! I always wanted to!

MOSUN: Meet them for what purpose?

EUGENE: That we are friends ; that I am the one looking after you.

MOSUN: But you know what I mean.

EUGENE: No, I don't know what you mean.

MOSUN: You are married. How do I tell my parents that I have been dating a married man?

EUGENE: Then let's get married.

MOSUN: You know that you don't mean that. You know that you can't take a second wife and I don't want to be a second wife as well!

EUGENE: I see...so you want out?

(*Silence*)

EUGENE: You want us to end this?

MOSUN: When the hammer meets the anvil there is no negotiation!

EUGENE: Mosun, tell me what you want; you know I love you. I can't afford to lose you.

MOSUN: Love? Are you sure? Are you sure you love me?

EUGENE: Yes I do. I love you; I really do. I want you forever. What I get from you, the comfort, the peace of mind, I can't get from my wife at home! But for the fact that our wealth comes from her family, I would have divorced her long ago.

MOSUN: You are getting the better of two worlds; I'm just floating between. I'm your *ashewo*, your spare tyre, your sex toy that you come and perform exotic sex styles with!

EUGENE: You an ashewo?

MOSUN: Yes your *ashewo*, a kept woman, a concubine!

EUGENE: Mosun!

MOSUN: What am I to you? What does an *ashewo* do? An ashewo sleeps with men for money.

EUGENE: But you don't sleep with men!

MOSUN: Yes, I don't sleep with men. I sleep with only you. But I sleep with you for material comfort. In a sense all kept women like me are *ashewo*.

EUGENE: My dear you are NOT *ashewo*.

MOSUN: Thank you for comforting me. I was attracted to you first time, even loved you because of your personality, your kindness, your handsomeness. But after I realized we could not marry I remained in the relationship because of the money, the material things you splashed on me.

EUGENE: Why are you so bitter Mosun? What has caused this?

MOSUN: Sometimes some people don't even have shit to shit.

EUGENE: What do you mean?

MOSUN: If a person does not have food to eat how can they shit?

EUGENE: Is that how you feel? I'm really sorry darling. Where did this bitterness sprout from?

MOSUN: Eugene, how many times have you taken me to the abortion table? Don't answer. Don't let these people in the auditorium laugh at my foolishness. I know how many times. How can you say that you love me and cannot let me have a child by you?

EUGENE: Mosun, please...

MOSUN: What manner of love is that?

EUGENE: You know we can't have a child outside wedlock!

MOSUN: I know. But listen to me. Do you know what it means
to bleed the life of a child out of my body? At thirty-two
years of age? Do you know? I have taken that route five
times in the last five years. Five abortions in five years!
May God forgive me! (*Sobs*) I don't want that anymore.
Perhaps I should have kept one of the pregnancies and
damned the consequence. But you always had your
reputation to consider; my emotions were and are
useless, inconsequential. I've been a fool; a big fool.

EUGENE: Mosun please don't talk like this. You are not a fool.
We have both enjoyed this affair!

MOSUN: I shouldn't talk? I should remain your lap dog? I know
that I am weak when it comes to calling off the
relationship. How many times have I woken up
resolved to end it all? How many? But when you call or
visit, I become weak. Why? Do you know how I feel
each time I go to church and the pastor rains curses on
women who have taken other women's husbands? I
shudder each time the pastor repeats the Seventh
Commandment – "*Thou shall not commit adultery*". I
feel like a leper breaking a rule which God expressly
said we must not obey.

EUGENE: Sometimes, we can't help breaking some rules...

MOSUN: Really? Do you know why we should end our relationship? If I get pregnant again, I will not, repeat, will not terminate the pregnancy.

EUGENE: But we can use protection...

MOSUN: How selfish can you be! What about me, my future, my life? I need my own man. Please go. Go and meet your rich wife. Leave this poor lady alone!

EUGENE: Just like that Mosun? You are ending this so abruptly without giving a thought to what we enjoyed before and what is ahead of us? Have I not been treating you right? Have I not met your demands?

MOSUN: That is what has kept me in this trap. You have spoilt me with money and affection. But Eugene, this is not love. You have kept me here just to satisfy your lust outside your matrimonial bed. That is the fate of all kept women – sex toys.

EUGENE: I think something is wrong somewhere. Go and dress up. Let's go out somewhere on the island for dinner and some drinks.

MOSUN: Sorry my dear. You can't get me this time. That's the old trick. We go out, have a nice time eating and drinking, we have sex and I forget myself. It is over now.

EUGENE: I see. I can't believe this is my Mosun.

MOSUN: Your Mosun is gone from your bed my big brother! This is a new Mosun...

EUGENE: Birds must return to their nests for safety my dear.

MOSUN: I like that image. Remember that some birds are caught by snares and never return. This bird has flown finally from your nest.

EUGENE: But you have not been caught!

MOSUN: You think so? I've been caught or is it liberated by the snare of conscience.

EUGENE: No no no!

MOSUN: Yes yes yes!

EUGENE: So you mock me now!

MOSUN: No. I can't ever mock you. You have been too good to me; your nest has been too comfortable for me. But it's an illusion.

EUGENE: It's our nest...

MOSUN: No, it's your nest Eugene; not mine. I don't belong there.

EUGENE: This is a new Mosun standing before me!

(Uncomfortable silence between them)

MOSUN: I'm expecting my friend Ochuko here at 4pm. She phoned to say she was coming.

EUGENE: Another time then? Say tomorrow? Can we take a trip to Abuja?

MOSUN: Thanks, but I cannot travel with you anymore.

EUGENE: Have you been nursing this for a long time? Only last week, we were together in the Meridian for the weekend. You gave no inkling at all that you were planning a coup.

MOSUN: A woman's heart is deep, my brother. But at the same time if you never gave my future a thought throughout the time then you don't really love me. Were I your sister would you encourage me to continue in a relationship that would get her nowhere? Would you?

EUGENE: But you are not my sister. Love is different, the circumstances are different.

MOSUN: Ah! Now I understand the kind of person you are.

EUGENE: It's okay. I will leave now. But just remember that I am a businessman. I expect returns on all my investments!

MOSUN: Eugene, you really said that? Is it the car you want? You want me to return it? I can give you the keys right away to buy my freedom. I can move out of this house by the weekend.

EUGENE: Don't misunderstand me. I didn't mean that. Sorry it came out that way, the wrong way. I will call again over the weekend when you have calmed down so that we may talk heart to heart. Love and anger do not lie in the same bed.

MOSUN: You are free to do as you wish.

EUGENE: I will return and take my sweetheart.

MOSUN: It's no use. Something deep inside me died today.

EUGENE: We have had a sweet relationship Mosun; don't throw everything away; don't throw those sweet days away.

MOSUN: Sugar is sweet my brother; but there comes a time when you no longer eat it without negative consequences. So you must quit eating sugar. I have reached that stage.

EUGENE: Love never dies; it can faint and can be revived. I will visit you again.

MOSUN: We once agreed that if the relationship had to end for any reason, we should part ways amicably. Do you remember?

EUGENE: I remember...

MOSUN: So you are free to visit.

EUGENE: But we have not parted ways. I shall return honey, I shall return. Just know that my feelings for you are undying. I will love you forever! I have completed your house at the estate in Ajah. Get ready to move in at the end of the month.

MOSUN: I'm not moving there. Please leave me alone. Leave meeeee!

(*He tries to kiss her good bye. She resists him. He takes his leave, storms out actually. Mosun locks the door and collapses into a chair and bursts into tears. She is in that condition for a few minutes. The song 'Yellow Bird' is playing in the background. She wipes her tears, takes a glass of water. She mounts a stool and brings down Eugene's picture that was on the wall. Breaks it. The phone rings. She picks it up.)*

MOSUN: Hello mom...I'm very fine. No. How is dad? .....Is he? That's fine. *(She listens to her mom for a while)* Okay mom. I will come home during the weekend and spend time with you.....Bye.

(There is a knock on the door. She shoves the broken picture under the chair)

MOSUN: Who is it?

VOICE: Your one and only!

MOSUN: A minute please. *(She wipes her face thoroughly before opening the door. She is suddenly bright and gay. She is now a different person)* O come in my dear *(They hug with passion. They kiss too)*

OCHUKO: How have you been?

MOSUN: I have been fine, I guess.

OCHUKO: Are you sure? I sense something in this house.

MOSUN: Have you become a rabbit that can sense things from a mile?

OCHUKO: How is Eugene?

MOSUN: That one, I guess he is fine.

OCHUKO: Guess? Have you not been in touch?

MOSUN: We have; he left here a few minutes ago.

OCHUKO: To avoid me?

MOSUN: Noooo. Why?

OCHUKO: Since he found out that I don't approve of your relationship he has been cold towards me.

MOSUN: I never noticed. Please forget about him. How's the home front, particularly your co-wife?

OCHUKO: (*They both burst into laughter*) She is fine. My senior mate! But Mosun, I am tired, just tired of everything.

MOSUN: I admire the courage and patience you have shown these many years. Do not give up at this late stage. She is getting old and I don't expect her to give you too much trouble much longer. Good a thing you guys have completed your house. You could move in there with the kids; your husband could then shuttle without offering any explanations to her.

OCHUKO: Sounds plausible; strange though.

MOSUN: Besides, she could pass on to greater glory!

OCHUKO: There's no glory where she will pass on to, what with the kind of wicked things that she does!

MOSUN: Pass on; whether to glory or damnation!

OCHUKO: I get the point. No such luck; there's longevity in their family.

MOSUN: Just join the *fall-down-and-die* people and your problems will be reduced!

(Laughter.)

OCHUKO: Expensive joke; but can you see what her atittude, her wickedness has driven us into?

MOSUN: It's not unusual. This world is a rat race, dog eat dog!

OCHUKO: The whole idea of making a joke out of praying for her to fall down and die!

MOSUN: Sad; yes very sad.

OCHUKO: The truth is that if she dies naturally, peace will be restored in the house. I will not wish her death but if she slumps and goes away I will be one of the happiest people around.

MOSUN: Then go the way of Option A!

OCHUKO: Which is?

MOSUN: Move to your new place without fanfare, without telling her!

OCHUKO: Do I have to sneak into my new house? I would feel terrible!

MOSUN: No need to feel terrible at all. Remember all the phases you went through in the marriage before you finally made your point?

OCHUKO: Are you telling me? How can I forget the first reason she gave for her son not to marry me? I remember that day like yesterday!

MOSUN: And when you returned from the bloodless battle you were happily sad!

OCHUKO: It was an eye opener for me. It was like drama, real life drama my sister.

MOSUN: And we were like actors on stage. You clearly recaptured the scene to me. I can still see it in my mind's eye.

(They switch into the roles of Mama Yellow and Onome. Mosun plays Mama Yellow while Ochuko plays Onome. With the proper change of accent, mannerisms and costume they role-play)

MAMA YELLOW: (*Mimics her manner of speaking*) This girl you are talking about, where does she come from?

ONOME: She is a Nigerian.

MAMA YELLOW: I'm a Nigerian too, but I come from Delta. I'm an Urhobo woman.

ONOME: She is a Yoruba lady.

MAMA YELLOW: Yoruba? Why is her name Ochuko?

ONOME: Her mother is Urhobo.

MAMA YELLOW: So you searched the whole of Delta, Bayelsa, Rivers and Edo States and you could not find a beautiful girl to marry? Is that what you mean?

ONOME: It's love; I love her.

MAMA YELLOW: Love! What kind of love?

ONOME: I know you very well; even if I introduced a lady from Rivers or Bayelsa you still would have chased them away? Why did you chase Tonye away? What about

Nonye? What of Eyesan? Even this one whose mother is Urhobo does not satisfy you.

MAMA YELLOW: Which part of Urhobo does her mother come from?

ONOME: Can you hear yourself Mama? Does it matter which part of Urhobo? The next minute you would say she is not from a good clan, not from a good family, or her mother is a witch. I'm fed up! You chased away all the nice girls I brought home!

MAMA YELLOW: Those girls were not properly brought up. I want the best for you.

ONOME: How do you know what is best for me?

MAMA YELLOW: I'm your mother; I should know.

ONOME: Or do you want to marry me?

MAMA YELLOW: God forbid! Hear the kind of big rubbish that is coming from your small mouth!

ONOME: What else do you expect me to say? May be you want us to live together all our lives, no intruder, no wife, no children.

MAMA YELLOW: How could you say that? Why won't I want grandchildren?

ONOME: I don't know!

MAMA YELLOW: Is that what you think?

ONOME: Yes...I bring this lady and you complain about her legs. I bring another, it's her complexion. Yet another, it's her family background! Then it's the way she greets you. You even complained that one was too thin! What about the one you said I should not marry because her skin was too black? You gave them derogatory nicknames. Mama, I'm not taking this from you anymore. Ochuko is my wife. So accept her!

MAMA YELLOW: Na wa! When did you become an army officer?

ONOME: You are a General in the Opposition Army and you gave birth to a General in the Rebel Army! A lion or lioness cannot give birth to a goat!

(*They burst into laughter and return to their real roles*)

OCHUKO: Mosun baby!

MOSUN: That's my name!

OCHUKO: That was how she was forced to accept me as a wife.

MOSUN: Battles all the way!

OCHUKO: Is it really worth it?

MOSUN: Is life not a battle? If there are no battles to be fought and won, how can we enjoy the world that we are in?

OCHUKO: You have a point there my sister; you do have a point. We have come a long way.

MOSUN: Yes, from secondary school through university. We have fought many battles.

OCHUKO: Thanks for being there for me.

MOSUN: You have been there for me in more ways than one.

OCHUKO: I remember those blissful moments! Gone forever!

MOSUN: Yes, gone forever, for our peace of mind.

OCHUKO: Old things have passed away.

MOSUN: As you know, I'd rather get into a marriage where I would fight battles and be a good wife than be the old spinster that I am gradually becoming!

OCHUKO: Mosun! We agreed that you must not give in to despondency!

MOSUN: I know. But you see, it's hard sometimes, very hard. One's parents, siblings, and old friends get involved one way or another. Some of the old friends start avoiding one because one has remained a spinster. You are the only one that has stuck with me.

OCHUKO: Mosun, you mean a lot to me, married or unmarried. A woman's worth is not defined by being tied to a man. A woman can find fulfillment in other things. If marriage does not come, then adopt a child and care for that child or have one biologically through a special arrangement.

MOSUN: I agree with you. Just that we have not reached that stage in our country.

OCHUKO: Some people have reached that stage; they don't care what people say. In Lagos there are many ladies who have taken the bull by the horn and have had children out of wedlock! The heavens did not fall!

MOSUN: Some have reached that stage yes. A lot depends on the family one comes from or the circumstances in the family.

OCHUKO: You are right. Perhaps I'm not the best person to preach this because I am fully and happily married.

MOSUN: One of the ironies of life.

OCHUKO: Yes. Do you remember how she harassed me before I got pregnant?

MOSUN: Who would forget that? No woman ever forgets the insults hurled at her because pregnancy isn't forthcoming. I know. My mother was a victim until I came. She told me the sad story and till date, you still find tears in her eyes each time she tells the story.

OCHUKO: On one of those bad days, Mama came visiting. I will never forget how she called me a decorative chair in the house.

MOSUN: I remember. You told me how you broke down and cried and cried and cried throughout the night. How you refused to be consoled by the words of comfort from your husband. How you felt abused and used by a fellow woman simply because she wanted another woman for her son.

OCHUKO: I look back now and laugh, though it was not funny when it happened. It's like an old wound. You scratch it and it gives a sweet sensation.

(They switch into role playing again between Mama Yellow and Ochuko. Mosun plays Mama Yellow while Ochuko plays herself)

MAMA YELLOW: Chuko!

OCHUKO: Yes ma!

MAMA YELLOW: Come here. I want to talk to you.

OCHUKO: Here I am ma

MAMA YELLOW: Look here may be your husband does not ask you the right questions. May be he thinks it's a joking matter. For how many years have you been married to my son now?

OCHUKO: Three years ma!

MAMA YELLOW: Three full years. Three years people of this world. Please listen. Three years and now, not even a pregnancy to show to the world that my son is a man!

OCHUKO: But Mama, you know it is not so!

MAMA YELLOW: What is not so?

OCHUKO: That there has been no pregnancy.

MAMA YELLOW: Where is the pregnancy?

OCHUKO: Three times now I have suffered miscarriages.

MAMA YELLOW: That is what we call story telling in Warri! I want a child period!

OCHUKO: But I am a fertile woman and I have had three pregnancies to show for it!

MAMA YELLOW: Three pregnancies! Where are the kids?

OCHUKO: I am waiting on God and my heavenly father will do it for me!

MAMA YELLOW: I want to see the effects of what my own son has been doing with you! When we came to see your family it was a woman we went to ask for; not a man who would simply decorate the sitting room or bedroom like a table.

OCHUKO: I'm a full-woman and I have gotten pregnant three times. So I am not a decorative object. When God's time comes I will produce a baby; not even a baby. I will produce babies.

MAMA YELLOW: That is what you ladies suffer. That is the punishment for performing multiple abortions before marriage while jumping from one bed to another

OCHUKO: Mama, I firmly reject your accusation. I never did one abortion in my life. If it is so easy why is it that you have only one child? Why didn't you produce ten? My mother had ten children. Ten!

MAMA YELLOW: So you must abuse me too now. I don't blame you. It is my foolish son that has carried and kept you in this house that I blame. People of the world see how my son's wife has heaped curses on me. My son must hear this. All I did was to ask her why she has not given birth and she poured insults on me.

(*They return to the present and burst into laughter*)

Mosun: Ochuks!

OCHUKO: Yes that's me.

MOSUN: That last one was hot. You made her cry too just as you cried later in the night.

OCHUKO: She reported the matter to my husband when he returned from work.

MOSUN: Like a second wife...

OCHUKO: Yes indeed, like a second wife. She was like a second wife who swore to kick me out of the marriage.

MOSUN: How did Onome react?

OCHUKO: When he asked me I recounted what actually happened. He simply advised me to avoid arguments with Mama and assured me of his love for me.

MOSUN: Of course he understood everything.

OCHUKO: What none of us knew at the time was that I was three months gone.

MOSUN: Three months gone and you didn't know!

OCHUKO: It confused me when the doctor confirmed my pregnancy.

MOSUN: How did it happen? By special arrangement? (*They both burst into laughter*)

OCHUKO: Truth was that I kept having light flows during the three months and I didn't know, didn't believe I was pregnant, even after the tests came out positive. I hid myself for six months, supported by my husband.

Before anyone knew it I was in a private hospital and had my baby safely!

MOSUN: The monitoring spirits failed in the assignment!

OCHUKO: Yes oo! My God blinded them during the period and set confusion in their midst.

MOSUN: Your husband was beside himself with joy. He bought drinks for everybody at the hospital that day.

OCHUKO: Then it was time for the next battle. First she hinted that she did not see my pregnancy. When that did not wash, she started complaining about the sex of the baby. That one's first child should be a boy.

MOSUN: She really had the guts to say that to you! Wonders will never end. Here was a woman who ought to understand the feelings of another woman, mocking her daughter-in-law for not producing a male child as first grandchild.

OCHUKO: That is what baffles me. When a woman is widowed, it is women in the man's family that subjects the widow to all kinds of indignities. They sometimes wash the corpse and ask the widow to drink the water to prove that she didn't kill her husband. In one particular area, the woman is left by the graveside of the late husband all alone for three nights. Women!

MOSUN: The things we do to ourselves! You remember what happened after you finally had a male child?

OCHUKO: That one? I remember. Her bias became very clear.

(They switch into Mama Yellow, Onome and Ochuko. Mosun plays Mama Yellow and Mosun. The action takes place in the house of Atumu. Ochuko has just returned from the hospital. There are guests in the house but the action is limited to Mama Yellow, Ochuko and Onome.)

OCHUKO: Here is my son, your grandson (*Handing over the baby to her*)

MAMA YELLOW: Welcome. Is this a boy or a girl?

OCHUKO: It's a BOY, Mama.

ONOME: It's a boy; your first grandson!

OCHUKO: You have always cried for a boy. God has finally answered your wish, answered my prayer to give my husband his own image.

MAMA YELLOW: (*Inspecting the baby closely, turning the baby up and down*) But he doesn't look like my son! He does not look like Onome!

ONOME: What do you mean?

OCHUKO: Are you saying we picked up the baby from the street?

MAMA YELLOW: I didn't say that.

OCHUKO: Or are you saying it's not your son that impregnated me?

MAMA YELLOW: God forbid; why should such a thought come to anybody's mind?

ONOME: Maama! Look at his nose!

OCHUKO: Look at his fingers!

ONOME: Look at his ears!

MAMA YELLOW: I will see things clearly when he grows up.

ONOME: Mama, I will not let you spoil my day. Give me my son and please go to the room while I entertain my guests.

MAMA YELLOW: I need to go and rest.

(Music. While dancing is on the scene goes to the present. Laughter between the two as usual)

OCHUKO: The things we have seen and the words we have heard!

MOSUN: Will write another book of two hundred pages!

OCHUKO: I've kept hoping that the woman would change; I thought seeing her grandchildren grow would change her. But no such luck, with each day she withdrew into herself.

MOSUN: It's possible hers was a psychological illness that needed treatment. But who can ever suggest that hereabouts?

OCHUKO: I can't even suggest that to my husband, loving as he is. To admit that his mother needs psychiatric evaluation! That would be the day!

MOSUN: You are right my sister. Although there are many people who need psychiatric attention going around today, they would never hear of visiting a psychiatrist. They would rather go to church and confess their problems...

OCHUKO: Yes, I agree. Our folks still attribute mental illness to the work of evil spirits. People who are exposed enough to see a psychiatrist for their problems do so in secret.

MOSUN: Mental illness is just like any other disease that can be cured. It comes in different forms you know.

OCHUKO: Are you telling me?

MOSUN: Ochuks!

OCHUKO: Yeah, what is it?

MOSUN: I broke up with Eugene today (*She bursts into tears. Ochuko consoles her*)

OCHUKO: It's okay baby; don't cry. You have taken the best decision. Be strong

MOSUN: Thanks

OCHUKO: I know it's not easy. But I assure you that true love will come your way. Just stay close to God.

MOSUN: I will. Ochuko, please never leave me.

OCHUKO: I promise; I will always be there for you just as you stood by me these many years.

MOSUN: Thanks, sister.

OCHUKO: I congratulate you my sister. Now you have closed a bad door, a good one will open. Be strong!

MOSUN: I don't know how I did it, but I did.

OCHUKO: When?

MOSUN: I called it off today.

OCHUKO: You went through all that today and still had the presence of mind to listen to my cries? Oh how selfish was I!

MOSUN: You are not selfish; you aren't at all. You sensed something was wrong and asked.

OCHUKO: I am so happy for you. Something good will happen now. Your real man will come into your life.

MOSUN: Amen.

OCHUKO: How did he take it?

MOSUN: He didn't take it well. He hasn't agreed that it's over. In fact, he promised to come here on Saturday to take me out.

OCHUKO: Don't go anywhere with him.

MOSUN: It will be tough, but I will try. Might just leave the house and switch off my mobile phone.

OCHUKO: You could actually come to my place...

MOSUN: No; I will spend the weekend at a retreat. Mom called today so I might just go over to the house and be a good girl. Indeed, I promised her that I would be coming over for the weekend.

OCHUKO: Excellent idea...

MOSUN: Thanks.

OCHUKO: My sister, it's almost 6.30pm. Let me head for the house before they send a search team to look for me.

I'm surprised that my husband has not called me. (*Just then her phone rings*) Talk of the angel...Hello! You are true son of your father. I just wondered aloud that you hadn't called me all evening and then the phone rang....... Yes, I've been with Mosun all evening! No..........Yes.........I'll be on my way now. Okay...bye for now. How the mind works?

MOSUN: Thank God that Onome has been faithful and strong. Marriage is not all bad as some people would have us believe.

OCHUKO: There are sweet moments; indeed there are more sweet moments than moments of horror.

MOSUN: Thanks for looking in and for being a friend indeed.

OCHUKO: It's you I should thank. Thanks for the comfort which our chats give me. As you have been there for me, may God and friends be there for you too!

MOSUN: Amen my sister.

OCHUKO: Bye for now. (*Ochuko hugs Mosun*)

MOSUN: Bye

(*Ochuko leaves. Mosun, pauses, stares into space in a reflective manner. Sadness and resignation on her face! Then she says*)

My heart is a soft house of sorrows; it has been for a long time. When it is afternoon and I swim in the sweet things of life, my spirit rises. At night, when I am all alone, just me inside this façade, this gift of love, happiness eludes me. But that must end now. From the remnants of the fall, I must build a house again.

(End of Scene)

Act Two

Scene One

(Onome is in a bar. A glass of beer is before him. Light is focused on him. The lines are his thoughts, but vocalized. So they should be delivered in that manner)

ONOME: She is my mother, yes, she is my mother. She gave me birth. She suffered while I was growing up; she really suffered. I remember like yesterday how she suddenly became a trader, this woman who had been an educated housewife, taken care of, pampered by her aged husband, how she took to the most menial of all trades and funded my life and my education and gave me a head start in life. She did not decide to travel to Cotonou to buy second hand clothes and other fast-moving items, the popular trading business for women at the time. The Cotonou trade though illegal, was more attractive, more financially rewarding. But she bought fish from the creeks and sold fish as a whole-trade businesswoman to people in the town. She spent nights and weeks in the mosquitoes and pirates-infested-creeks; weeks of no contact with us who were left in the hands of her teenage niece. Do you know what trading in dry fish means? It means the smell of fish all around her any time you met her. Our house smelt of fish. Our clothes smelt of fish. Our bathrooms smelt of fish. Even my school uniforms smelt of fish. I don't want to recall the teasing I suffered in the hands of my school mates over fish smell. It's not a pleasant memory. It wasn't a pleasant smell. It was not. It was nothing we could be proud of. But the smell of fish in the house meant money; meant there was food to eat, there was money to pay the fees of her two children, and there was money to support her niece who lived with us. As they say in Sapele, currency notes, particularly old currency notes, have a bad smell; but old smelly currencies do powerful things too. So, I appreciate everything; I appreciate her sacrifice, her years of toiling to fund my education. I love her, I respect her, and I owe her an obligation. I have honoured her all my life. And I want to continue to honour her.

The good old book says we should *"honour our parents in the Lord, for this is right",* it is the first commandment with a promise. I have no doubt that she loves me intensely. But she loves me so in a destructive way; not intended though. She wants to possess me, body and soul, to own me, to keep me within her orbit all the time. I sympathize with her. I understand her. I understand that she lost my sister shortly after we completed secondary school. I understand the tragic circumstances, how an electric cable struck down by lightning hit Omare my only sister, my only real sibling, as she played in school. I became her only prized possession. It's a kind of mental disorder, I believe, though I haven't done any research into it. But she wants to ruin my marriage; she is simply overbearing and suffocating. She behaves like a bad second wife in the house.

Sometimes I feel like running away from the house. It's that bad. Whenever I suggest getting her, her own accommodation she falls sick and she ends up in the hospital. And I pay huge bills. I feel sorry for my dear wife; she has borne the brunt of my mother's extreme aggression. I love my wife, I love my mother, and I love my children. But my mother who loves me does not love my wife, does not love my children. My wife loves me, loves our children but cannot love my mother because my mother doesn't want her love. How complex life can be! Wish she would just show some love; there would be a sudden transformation of things in the house, in my world. Sometimes, when it gets too, too tough at home, I run here and enter the green bottles with friends. The sad news is that whenever the effects of the green bottles wear off, I return to the same nightmare. But a moment of temporary ease is better than living a life of permanent stress. Today I am meeting Jerry my old school mate and friend. We have weathered storms together in the past. He is a bit rascally and though I do not agree with his extreme views all the time, he is a good person to talk to. I have questions and I need answers. I have questions for myself which I must answer. I have questions which he should help me to answer before I take any action. I need to take an action, take some actions.

(Jerry enters. The lights become full and the reflective Onome springs into his ebullient self.)

ONOME: Man Jerry!

JERRY: Man Nomsky! How are you boy?

ONOME: I'm sweet. You?

JERRY: I'm dying for a drink

ONOME: Thanks for showing up at such short notice.

JERRY: Thanks? Why? I should thank you for the invitation. How can I resist a bottle of beer while discussing the world with an old pal?

ONOME: You know it's not the beer; it's the things that flow between us.

JERRY: Okay Mr. Philosopher Sir. Let the beer flow.

ONOME: Bar man!

JERRY: Tomide!

VOICE: On my way Sir.

(Tomide enters with two bottles of beer and glasses.)
ONOME: Good boy.

TOMIDE: Good evening Sir

JERRY: Good evening. A very good boy he is. He sure knows our brands.

TOMIDE: Thank you Sir!

JERRY: Take a drink on us!

TOMIDE: Thank you Sir. But I no dey drink beer Sir.

JERRY: Take a malted drink.

TOMIDE: Thank you Sir!

(*He moves into the background. They pour their beers, clink glasses and after a swig the discussion starts*)

ONOME: How are things?

JERRY: We are forging ahead. How's the home front?

ONOME: That's one of the reasons I called you. I'm getting to breaking point! I recall a poem which I read many years ago. Its words started coming back to me recently, haunting me. I didn't really understand it then; I do now! I took time to copy it before coming over:

(*Reading*)

> *I have no mouth or tongue*
>
> *For the elder who scatters the family*
>
> *With rotten smelly words*
>
> *Like the foul fart of a fat fool*
>
> *Who ate ogwo isha the night before*

JERRY: That's deep! Only God knows what tragedy befell the poet to evoke such a vote of no-confidence on the elders!

ONOME: Sometimes the depth of evil is so great that a blind man can see it!

JERRY: Things must be really serious for you to be at breaking point after managing the situation so well these many years.

ONOME: Managed the situation so very well! At what costs? My blood pressure is permanently high. Saw my doctor yesterday, because I felt dizzy. He asked if there was anything in particular bothering me. He gave me a checklist to tick off; how I felt about them. On the list were such items as job satisfaction, domestic peace, trouble from in-laws, parents, net income, career prospects, etc. You know the usual stuff.

JERRY: Who doesn't?

ONOME: I failed domestic peace and parents' wahala. He said I should reduce stress level as much as possible and exercise all the time. I then said to myself that I must not die suddenly and leave my kids to suffer the same fate I had to endure as a boy.

JERRY: Well, if your health is receiving such an attack, we have to develop another strategy for survival.

ONOME: I thought so.

JERRY: What ideas do you have?

ONOME: What are my options? That's why I'm here.

JERRY: Options? Hmmmmmmm!

ONOME: Why the long pause?

JERRY: Tough, very tough. Let me tell you a story. Once there lived a man who had two wives. The first one was good, friendly and possessed all the virtues a true wife should have. Sadly, she had no children. She then arranged for a second wife for her husband. Indeed, she paid the bride price and the new wife was referred to as the first wife's wife. The man enjoyed it all. He had the best of two worlds, so to speak. All the kids which the second wife bore belonged to the first wife. Of course their husband was the father of the kids. Everything worked until the seventh year when ladies from the age-grade of the second wife started putting ideas into the second wife's head. Why must you be the one to go to the stream and fetch water for a cripple? Why must you be married to a woman? I won't take that nonsense. This went on and on until one day the second wife insulted the first wife in the presence of her husband. She didn't expect the kind of reaction which she received from her husband. He so beat her that the entire community came to beg him. He asked the second wife to leave the house immediately. The first wife, kind and trusting joined the team to beg the husband. This softened his heart. He then re-considered his decision and reinstated the rude wife. Six months after the pardon, the first wife died suddenly. It was later confirmed that she was poisoned by the second wife. At this stage it was communal justice that was visited on the offending woman. But a soul had been lost!

ONOME: Hmmm! So where do I come in here?

JERRY: Take a pick!

ONOME: I don't have time for riddles.

JERRY: I understand. Your life is already a riddle.

ONOME: You can say that again.

JERRY: The elders did not say that a bee perched on the scrotum should be left there; they simply advise that we should shoo it away gently.

ONOME: I'm listening.

JERRY: You and Mama have to part ways now, for the sake of your family and your health.

(A long silence...)

ONOME: (*A deep sigh*) Hard road to travel...

JERRY: The process of disengagement could and should be worked out!

ONOME: I may need to involve Mama's pastor...

JERRY: Good. What is the proposal?

ONOME: We will tell her that we've completed our house

JERRY: That would be good news to her!

ONOME: The bad news would be that she cannot and should not move in with us.

JERRY: What reason would you give?

ONOME: I don't know yet; just thinking on my feet.

JERRY: We have made progress. A decision has been taken

ONOME: Yes, a decision has been taken, good or bad!

JERRY: Better to take a bad decision than to remain in limbo..

ONOME: Yeah...hopefully, it's the best for everybody.

JERRY: Let's drink to that; the details will be worked out or things will just sort themselves out.

(They clink glasses. Lights out)

Act Two

Scene Two

(This scene starts outside the Atumu House. It takes place inside the auditorium between Rev. Father Raymond and Onome. As much as possible, they try to get the audience involved.)

ONOME: I do not need to go into the details of our problem because you are very familiar with it. I have reached a decision. For the sake of my health and the continued survival of my family, I need to provide a separate residential accommodation for Mama.

FATHER RAYMOND: I see...

ONOME: I need to break the news to Mama and I would like you to be present. In fact, if you can help me to prepare her mind I'd be grateful.

FATHER RAYMOND: What's the plan?

ONOME: It's a bit complex. You see, all the while she kept putting me under pressure to build a house we had already started developing our property.

FATHER RAYMOND: God be praised!

ONOME: It is time to move to the new house. I also believe it is time to give Mama her accommodation.

FATHER RAYMOND: With God all things are possible.

ONOME: How will she take the news that she can't move in with us to the new place? That's my worry.

SOMEONE-IN-THE-AUDIENCE: Your family comes first!

FATHER RAYMOND: What exactly do you have in mind?

ONOME: I believe the time has come for me to reduce the stress levels in my life. During my last medicals, I was diagnosed with high blood pressure. The doctor advised me to reduce the stress in my life and embark on regular exercise. I'm tired of being woken up at odd hours for lectures and poke-nosing and denigrating my wife. I'm tired of having a mother in the house who wouldn't accept my children, who has remained hostile to them from birth; a mother who refused to carry my babies after they were born. It is affecting me and it is affecting my wife; we have managed to avoid any serious quarrels in spite of potentially explosive situations.

FATHER RAYMOND: You want me to break the news to her that you have built your house and that you are ready to move.

ONOME: Exactly!

FATHER RAYMOND: It's possible to handle the matter in another way.

ONOME: Any advice would be welcome Father.

FATHER RAYMOND: Don't you think you should get her another place first before moving?

ONOME: Why, if I may ask?

FATHER RAYMOND: The fact that you are moving into your house and she is not allowed to move in there might be more debilitating. Think about it.

ONOME: I guess you are right.

FATHER RAYMOND: Let us tell her that you have found a new and comfortable place for her...

ONOME: Okay!

FATHER RAYMOND: We will tell her hat you would get her a nanny to stay with her. Give her all the things to make her comfortable.

ONOME: It's okay. Might be a better option Father. That's why I thought I should get you involved.

FATHER RAYMOND: By the way, there is a vacant apartment in the compound where I live; you know it is owned by the church. There are mothers like her who live there. It might soften the impact on her, the impact of separation.

ONOME: I'm happy you know the depth of things between us.

FATHER RAYMOND: I'm a man of prayers. Your mother's link with, link to you is more than ordinary. To her the umbilical cord was never severed; that's how she feels. Whenever you are sick, she falls ill too. I won't say it's healthy neither can I condemn it. It's almost mystical. If she wasn't a woman that I trusted, I would have thought there was a covenant between both of you.

ONOME: I'm also puzzled. Father Raymond, the bible talks about loving one's neighbour, love being a fulfilling of the law. But is there any such thing as destructive love, love which consumes people?

FATHER RAYMOND: Any feeling which consumes is not love as far as the Bible is concerned; love is perfect and it is without strife.

ONOME: How do we then describe the feeling which my mother has for me as love?

FATHER: Let's put it this way: your mom's feeling or attachment to you is a psychological reaction to the loss which she suffered at a point in her life. She needs to be evaluated by a psychologist and put through some therapy. She is an example of what psychologists call a 'narcissistic mother'. As a man of faith, I can pray with her, pray for her for God Almighty to ease her of the tension. With God all things are possible.

ONOME: But Father, you have prayed all these years; why has there been no change?

FATHER: My prayer needs to be complemented by the work of a psychologist or vice versa.

ONOME: Thanks Father for being so forthright.

FATHER: How? What do you mean?

ONOME: I have in mind the Pentecostal pastors and miracle workers who preach that they could pray problems away through astounding miracles!

SOMEONE0-IN-THE-AUDIENCE: Prayer is the master key!

FATHER RAYMOND: May be that's their gift. I won't judge
them; the good book says that judge not so that you
may not be judged. But the ministry of Christ which I
represent combines the spiritual with the physical to
receive healing. If a miracle happens along the way, we
ascribe it to the goodness of God, not our power.

(*They have been on the move since the discussion started. Now
they have arrived at The Atumus' House. Mama Yellow is in the
sitting room*)

MAMA YELLOW: Welcome to my home. Good to see you here
today Father. I heard you came to the house but by the
time I came out I was told that you had taken a walk
with Onome. How are you Father?

FATHER RAYMOND: I'm grateful to God for life.

MAMA YELLOW: Your walk was very long!

ONOME: When you are chatting with Father, you are never
conscious of time, you know.

MAMA YELLOW: The matter must have been important...

FATHER RAYMOND: O yes. We had to have a heart to heart talk
in a clean and healthy environment.

MAMA YELLOW: What do we get you to drink or eat?

FATHER: I am fine. Thanks Mama. I will have my next meal at 7pm, my doctor's advice.

MAMA YELLOW: It's okay. It's good to respect a doctor's advice.

FATHER RAYMOND: Yes, particularly competent doctors.

MAMA YELLOW: I hope there is no problem?

FATHER RAYMOND: Not at all. Onome wanted counseling and I obliged him.

MAMA YELLOW: Thank you for being there for us.

FATHER RAYMOND: It's a pleasure to serve the body of Christ. Mama we need to talk.

MAMA YELLOW: I hope nobody has died, Father! Please, tell me...

FATHER RAYMOND: No such thing.

MAMA YELLOW: Onome, is everything alright?

ONOME: Yes.

MAMA YELLOW: I hope you were not sacked or retired?

ONOME: No Mama, not at all.

MAMA YELLOW: So, what is it?

FATHER RAYMOND: I have come to advise that you need to move into a special accommodation, your own accommodation.

MAMA YELLOW: So, someone really died!

FATHER RAYMOND: Nobody has died, Mama.

(*Silence. Background music of Jim Reeves –Pa Ayers*)

FATHER: Mama!

   (*Silence*)

ONOME: Mama

   (*Silence, then after a few minutes*)

MAMA YELLOW: Onome! Is this your decision?

ONOME: Mama, please accept this in good faith. We have secured a decent place for you in the compound where Father lives. I have also hired a maid to assist you in your daily chores.

MAMA YELLOW: So I will now go to the market, buy foodstuff and make my own food, sleep on my own, live alone.

ONOME: But Mama, you have always insisted on buying your own stuff and preparing your food and living separately even while living with us. This is merely to...

FATHER RAYMOND: Mama, you see, the constant quarrels in the house and the tension have had an effect on the health of your son. He now has high blood pressure and as you know, this is dangerous...

MAMA YELLOW: So I am the cause of the high blood pressure! Onome, are you saying my stay in this house has given you high blood pressure?

ONOME: The doctor says I should reduce my stress level if not I would drop dead. I appeal to you to accept the arrangement. The place is beautiful and just be assured that I will always visit you and spend quality time with you.

MAMA YELLOW: It is well. When do you want to throw me out?

ONOME: No one wants to throw you out.

FATHER RAYMOND: At the end of this month you can move into your new home where I will be your neighbour.

MAMA YELLOW: It will be nice to have you as my neighbour; it means that I will always have prayers said for me every day and every night. Is the place ready?

ONOME: Not quite.

MAMA YELLOW: When will the place be ready?

ONOME: If we have your permission then I can furnish the place before Friday.

MAMA YELLOW: There is no need for permission to be granted.

FATHER RAYMOND: We care for you; no matter what happens, we....

MAMA YELLOW: Onome, from what you have said, I do not have a choice in the matter. If I continue to stay here in your house, you will die.

ONOME: Mama, I hope you are not...

MAMA YELLOW: I'm not a child. I'm your mother; I understand how things work. I would rather die than allow my stay in your house give you high blood pressure that could kill you.

ONOME: Don't say things like that...

MAMA YELLOW: Things like what? You have said it clearly that I am the one killing you.

ONOME: No Mama; it's not you. It's stress.

MAMA YELLOW: I have become a witch that wants to kill her only son!

ONOME: Not so Mama; you are not a witch. No one has called you a witch, God forbid.

FATHER RAYMOND: Sister Yellow; you are taking this too far. I decided to be part of the discussions to assure you that Onome has no evil plans. If you love him truly, the time has come to for you to go your separate ways.

M AMA YELLOW: Yes, I am ready to move to my own place now, to separate from my son. Nothing lasts forever, good or bad.

FATHER RAYMOND: I am happy that you feel this way!

MAMA YELLOW: I hope after I have moved in as your neighbour I will not be accused of trying to kill you too Father?

FATHER RAYMOND: No such thing Mama, No such thing! Our compound, as you have rightly observed is a place of prayer. You will have neighbours, people of your age and younger ones who are of the same faith. You will be fully engaged in church work.

MAMA YELLOW: When the spirit which takes a man to the other land arrives for his assignment while he is driving a car, the airbag simply aids the flight.

FATHER RAYMOND: Though the other world is better we do not determine when we take our exit from here. It's only the Almighty Father that knows.

MAMA YELLOW: Sometimes the journey can be quickened by man.

FATHER RAYMOND: It is not for man to do; that would be playing God.

MAMA YELLOW: It is well my son. I will move on Friday.

FATHER RAYMOND: God bless you. It is in the interest of everybody. God bless you Mama! Let us pray! Prayer time! Onome, call your wife and children.

ONOME: Ochuko love! Sweety pie! Ese, Andy and Harriet. It's prayer time; Father Raymond wants you all here now.

(Ochuko and the children all come in and take part in the prayer. Throughout the prayer, Mama Yellow remains passive, eyes open, detached from the spirit of prayer. She is introspective, gone beyond the present. Father Raymond and Onome kneel in supplication, eyes closed and do not really see her countenance or her posture).

FATHER RAYMOND: O Lord God of Heaven and earth, the God of peace, the God of harmony, the God of unequalled wonders, the God of Families, God of Mothers, the God of Children! I call on you today in all humility. I praise your name o great God. I thank you for harmony in families, I thank you for peace, I thank you for life. I thank you for making that which appears difficult to be simple. Today we have entered a new course in this family. We have agreed to stay in different houses yet in one home, one home guided by God. We pray you God Almighty to make this possible. We pray that the union of spirit between mother and son continue to grow. May your peace reign in this house! Bless Mama!

ALL: Amen!

FATHER RAYMOND Bless Onome!

ALL: Amen

FATHER RAYMOND: Bless Ochuko!

ALL: Amen

FATHER RAYMOND: Bless the children!

ALL: Amen!

FATHER RAYMOND: In the name of our Lord Jesus Christ!

All: Amen!

FATHER RAYMOND: Mama I will be glad to have you as my neighbour in the Lord's house.

MAMA YELLOW: Thank you. Father we shall meet in my Father's house where there are
many mansions. I will be glad to be your neighbour as from Friday.

FATHER RAYMOND: Bless you Mama. I'm off. Bye for now.

MAMA YELLOW: Bye bye!

(*Mama Yellow remains in one position, sitting and staring into space. She does not respond to any motions. Father and Onome move towards the door and Onome sees off the priest. Ochuko waves Father Raymond goodbye. She goes into the room with her children. Onome returns from seeing off his mother, attempts to talk to her, but she is still, obviously not ready for any small talk. He goes into his bedroom. After a few seconds Mama comes alive in that same calm manner*)

MAMA YELLOW: I am going to bed to close my old weary eyes; if in the morning my legs refuse to come down from the bed, do not look for my spirit in a faraway place. No one can take my earth from me!

SOMEONE-IN-THE-AUDIENCE: *Oma se o!*

(*As she goes into the room, the light goes off*)

Postscript

(The Bishop's Court. Father Raymond comes into the Court Scene as in the Prologue and takes a seat. The Bishop comes in and takes the position of a Judge who is ready to give a verdict. Father Raymond rises and bows in deference)

BISHOP: Father Raymond, I find you............ NOT GUILTY!

(A sudden burst of music in reaction to the verdict compels all members of the cast to dance on to the stage; Mama Yellow and Ochuko and Onome hold hands. Father Raymond joins them, beaming with smiles and shaking hands with everyone)

The End

-

Printed in the United States
By Bookmasters